Powers of Petals

ISBN: 979-8-9926258-3-7 (paperback)
ISBN: 979-8-9926258-4-4 (hardback)

Certified under US Copyright Office in accordance with title 17

American Library of Congress Number (LCCN): 2025913834

This is an original work of fiction. All references to historical events, real places and real people are used factiously. All characters, organizations and events portrayed in this novel are either a product of the author's imagination or used fictitiously.

Front Cover Image by Tatenda Thumba

www.JosephMukai.store

First edition 2025.

Joseph&Mukai Business
1849 South Road, #1017,
Wappinger Falls, NY 12590

Powers of Petals

Urban and Townships Lyrics
By
Mukai Heather Jaravaza

Table of Contents

The Birthing

A wretched scream
invades Night's darkness.
The woman bites
into Wind's breath. She shudders
in pain, scrambles, and runs.
Tears trail down her form.
Desperately, she pushes.
Water gushes out of her innermost parts.
Yesterday, this time, God birthed her.
He molded and created her.

Today, on the seventh day, life began.
Beneath the confusion of the past,
she found herself
resting on the other side of norm,
discovered herself hidden away
from the sword of criticism. Captured
beyond the confines of expectation.
Today, she saw herself—God's divine creation.
She fell into a trance,
because the woman He birthed
is beautifully beautiful.

Johnny's Gone

Johnny's gone!
He forgot to say goodbye or pay this month's rent,
but Johnny remembered to grab his guitar—
and steal our savings, too.
Snuck out of our bed,
left in the dark hours of Saturday night.
Late enough so I'd wait till Monday
before I called Renaissance Bank.
Johnny ran like the wind,
defying space and time,
carrying his many dreams wrapped in stolen cash.
Street dreams of unyielding fame—
fast cars and hit songs.
He scurried
to catch the midnight train to Bulawayo,
and transfer in Musina.
Johnny crossed the border into his promised land.

A fat lady in her fifties wearing a dress
made for a girl in her twenties
came. She knocked on my door
two nights later.
Her golden stilettos crushed the kitchen floor
and my dignity, too!
"I've come to get Johnny's things."
The old woman giggled.

"What things? We lived together
but I brought it all!"
I defiantly pointed to this
and that.

"Johnny's gone!" Her plush lipstick reassured me.
"So, give me his things," the edges of her lips curled triumphantly,
"He'll need them for our wedding -
 next week in Johannesburg."

Johnny's Back

He comes crying.
Two years later!
Mumbling about how the big city shattered
his dreams, crushed,
his confidence as well.
"Where's my money, Johnny?"
"The big city swallowed that, too!"

Sighs
before removing his worn-out shoes.

"Where's the fat lady in the little girl's dress?
You know, the one
who came for your things?"

"She found her dream
and a younger man, too."
He takes off his tattered jacket,
drops it on my floor. "Left me
before we reached the altar in Johannesburg."

Johnny reaches for a half-empty glass
on the kitchen counter,
gulps
and picks up my embroidered napkin—
unfolds it,
a soft curse.
He wipes glistering sweat
gathering on his forehead.

Further, he walks in and settles
into the rocking chair that was once
his.

"Can't sit there, Johnny."

"Why?"

A whisper,
a giggle. "That seat belongs
to Mikey now."

Someone Else's

A woman stole someone else's husband,
and named him Love.
She wore a wedding dress discarded outside
Hunter's Thrift Store, and a pair of shoes, snatched
off her sister's floor.
Two sizes too small!
But sufficient
for the brief ceremony in a borrowed hall.

A year later,
The woman desperately escaped that marriage
Packing her few belongings—
things she'd purchased with someone else's paycheck.
Fleeing out of the back porch,
she climbed over a white picket fence,
and begged her neighbor for a place to stay.
The following morning, she moved in,
and called it her own.
In the winter, the woman knocked on an office door
pleading for a job.
By spring, she sat in the interviewer's chair—
She stole that, too!

Fall came, and seasons changed.
The company replaced the woman
with a recruiter with "appropriate credentials."
The neighbor changed his locks
and threw out the woman's scant belongings—
a pair of worn-out wedding shoes, an overdue library book,
and her grandmother's missing pearls hidden
in a borrowed suitcase!

She waded through the darkness,
hungry, wrapped
in refurbished hand-me-downs,

struggling to hide her shame from the world she'd played with,
seeking shelter in any man's arms.
A faint protection from the story of her past,
desolate yet unapologetic.
A woman with many nothings,
because everything she owned
was always someone else's something.

Cry of Pink Roses

I met him once.
"The Cry of Pink Roses."
Beneath a thirsty summer evening,
he appeared.
In the curtains of Night's veil,
I witnessed the dazzle
of his bright, pearly smile.
It was enough!
I followed him
into the murky confessions of that day
through the dark, secluded alley of October's uncertainty.

He took me in circles before I understood
the endlessness of their journey.
Into a maze of deserts
and wasted water wells, I followed.
Suddenly, in a glimpse,
he was gone. An empty memory!
I sat in the silence of a drought-baked field
surrounded by forgotten trees
amid forsaken soil.
And when I looked up again,
there he was,
lurking in the dark secret places.
smiling at another girl!
I heard an old woman whisper his name.
"Beware."
A warning!

The Window Shopper

Slowly,
she wades through the snow
adding the memory of her mark
to footsteps gone before her.
Purposefully, her weary feet tread the darkness
onward and onward
toward waves of light bursting through glass walls.
Her small frame stands in a familiar place: the space
between the glass window and a deteriorating brick wall.
Forgetting her weary shoes and moth-bitten coat,
her chaffed hands rest on the windowpane.
Hidden in darkness, the girl's eyes dance
at the sights before her.
In the warmth of Goodies Home Store,
a man in a three-piece suit carefully conceals his calloused hands.
Grinning at his daughter's delighted squeal,
he hands her a piece of Goodies chewing candy.
The other hand slides a silver perfume tin
into his wife's bosom.
In the next aisle, a new bride blushes.
Her slender fingers trail over delicate leaves
of lazy underwear.
A farmer roars in laughter, frantically encircling
the display of Deer tractors.
Smiling, the girl at the glass window turns away,
her weary feet trailing through melting snow.
"I'll be back tomorrow,
again and again,
until one day, I, too, can enter Goodies Home Store."

Courage's Feet

Making a pact with courage
to fight fear together
is the only road to success.
There I stand,
in the doorway of my existence,
the space between death and life—
in crevices separating yesterday from tomorrow.
An entry point into the house of infinite
possibilities, I stand.
But Man has made his own rules.
Man's pride comes
before a fall.
I stand
while the world challenges "mine."
At times, even I, too, must be brave,
rise,
and seek my goal, not guided
by the opinions and actions of "knowing men"
building mazes of confusion hidden
in rules and regulations.
Tonight, I am forced
to make a decision—
that even if the plant I've nurtured
in this house of possibilities
dies due to my ways,
I must be ready to plant
another. For if I refuse to go
further through the doorway of life
then forever I will be here,
and unlike those (successful and unsuccessful)
who've made their pact with courage,
I will die
unsung,
alone,
in fear.

Mirage

We ran
barefoot battling scorching sand
through endless desert dunes.
Strangers!
She and I
never seeing one another but racing in the same direction
toward an oasis,
that sea of hope in a barren wasteland.
"Only one can enter," the scorching sand's judgement raged.
Yet we ran, she and I,
never knowing each other but fighting against time.

Alas, I stumbled,
fell onto caked dry earth
Despair pierced my twisted ankle.
Petals of blood trickled
out of broken skin. Stopped
by a west wind, I lay in confusion.
Then I saw her.
Never looking back, the girl ran faster.
Drenched in triumphant laughter,
spinning in victory, she leaped
into the sparkling waters of the oasis.
But alas! It was a mirage—
a compost heap amid the desert.
Wading through the murky stench,
the girl wailed in agony. Struggling
writhing in desolation,
she reached through the foul manure
to pull me in too.
But I was already gone,
taken by the wind
to Paradise's rain garden.

Sweeter than Love

Ain't nothing sweeter than new love.
Sweet smelling,
succulent,
scent-drenched like a spring rainfall
Wild blossoms
dancing in the wind while flowing through time.
New love is deliciously carefree
and irresistibly careless.

Healing the brokenhearted
and crumbling ancient strongholds,
new love shatters prison doors
and sets the lonely free.
Old men become strong again
while young men stagger
in love's drunken aroma.
Where there was a desert, love becomes an oasis,
a well of hope to aging widows.
Love transforms yesterday's spinsters
into giggling girls.
Restoring,
resurrecting,
making the impossible possible again.
In a world plagued by uncertainties,
there's truly nothing sweeter than new love.

A Recipe Called Love

Crisp, dripping honey.
Sweet,
Edible spring flowers.
A scoop of strong wrapped in the whisper
of surrender—five delicate petals
of contentment.
A dribble of salty rain tears,
submerged in the sweat of time.

Fold in a slab of mischief.
Moisten with laughter,
grease with cherry tart patience.
Soak overnight in forgiveness,
ripen with trust.
Together, we created a food
called love.

A Blues Quartet for Butterflies

He's come,
flaunting himself like sugarcane
in fields of corn.
Winter's gone.
Summer snuck in,
and he seeped into my secret places.

Whistling,
he meandered
down the long winding road,
leaned over and whispered into my form:
a sound,
a song.
Honey acoustics draped in eternal promises,
a melody I should know.

Holding the sun,
he ran with the wind,
painting my name on the hunger of his heart.
He looked into my all and wrapped it in his—
fed me laughter,
and I became unlocked!

Love's come knocking on my quiet
honey acoustic lyrics on a star-soaked night.
I see him.
Like spring morning dew,
he's standing at the gate,
waiting
to enter my garden and settle in my familiar.

Funny Love

Where does Love run to?
In the confines of midnight's hour,
where does my love rest his head?
Does he flow soft as the Zambezi
or roar like Victoria's waterflows?
Parading himself like summer's lightning,
will Love consume me?

Where does Love hide himself?
In the shadows of the day's delight,
exposing petals of promise
amid delicate raindrops.
Will Love find me in my secret place?
Will Love consume me?

A Woman's Purse

In this bag I carry
my purpose,
hidden in the folds of a crinkled magazine.
Within this purse, I carry
the last three dollars before my lights got cut off!
Two college degrees,
and a rejection letter from yesterday's interview,
a picture of my mother laughing and my daughter dancing,
the keys to my home—my shelter—
and an old subway card.
I clutch this bag and hold onto my dreams
while weaving through a flood of strangers
rushing to their own destinies.

A handkerchief to wipe my sister's tears.
Chocolate to console my lover's heart.
I'm still holding it all
when I'm falling with this bag
crushed by life's unyielding demands.

Did You and I?

Did I leave you?
Or did you close the door
before I finished speaking?
We met on the quiet end of Karigamombe Street
in the season of purple Jacaranda blossoms.
A chance meeting interrupting planned existences.
I gave you my story,
and you showed me your pain.
We danced through the storms.
Our journey, a river of laughter.
Fruitful promises
washed in the birth of possibilities,
an ancient duet for eternal love
Did you leave me?
Or did I close the door
before you finished the chapter of our journey?

Glitters of gold
The enticement of fame.
Neither tasted as good
as our moment. Remember
that night we fell apart.
It came in the form of a whirlwind
interrupting the solace of our love.
Did we leave us?
Or did the world close the door
before we completed our moment?

Nighttime

When you ignored me
I continued to smile.
When you left me,
I understood.
You mocked me,
and I excused it.
Now you blame me
for the things lost.
Vanished hope,
a cry for yesterday's expectations, your words shatter
hastily trampling over the cabin we built—
a hiding place,
the birthplace of our joy.
Today, I will quietly walk away.
Tomorrow, you will remember me –
your warm retreat in a cold and empty world.
Tomorrow is another life,
a new tune to the whistler.
Without you, I will live this life
and live it well.
Because the night I left you,
even the stars forgot to shine.

What Ifs

Endless stairs—
Cracked,
disturbed squares.
The man staggers down
a winding white brick stairwell.
His eyes search the dancing sea,
or maybe the waters are watching him.

Skin glistening,
caked white sand wrapped in forgotten sweat,
he stumbles onto muddy seashores
and stares at the Ship of Hope on the horizon.
Crawling—fingertips tunnel
under rhythmic caresses of a murky sea.
Further and further,
he reaches for the horizon,
but halts in the shadows of gray water banks.

Lost dreams,
Forgotten purpose.
Drunk with salty reality
and crippled by regret.
A man with a multitude of "what ifs,"
his reflection floats in the sea's melodic ripples
Body withered from building
wayward bridges that led to nowhere.
He bitterly laughs at the raging sea.
"Please wait for me."
 Unhindered desperation.
"Wait for me!" he screams at an indifferent sun
setting in the distance.
"What if?" The birthplace
of too many men's regrets.

Circle of Life

There is a time in life when your heart is truly lonely,
yet no one fits the position to fill it.
That time was 'then' for me
when dry grass gave birth to splintered seeds,
and new life—
sweet green emeralds between thistles and thorns.
I lay in the dark,
eyes open wide,
and saw the heart.
I am afraid
that life is like a circle
and nothing ever passes away—
over and over again, the circle cycles
until tomorrow becomes like yesterday:
waking and running,
sleeping,
praying,
eating,
waiting,
laughing and searching,
falling before crying,
empty heart dying.
After all, life is like a circle
and in the end, only rain remains.

Beautiful in Brooklyn

French patisserie shoved in the corner
of a crumbling brownstone.
Drums shouting into Battery Park.
Melodies of jazz on a rainy Thursday afternoon.

"Now," a shirtless boy taunts,
and Time starts rolling.
The sun rises,
jumps,
twists,
then turns to the sounds of mud drums.

"Open!" the shirtless boy screams.
Time surrenders but is still running
again and again,
until my blacks become grays,
and the dance within me concludes
in careful footsteps.
My quick grows into steady stability,
years rush past,
yet I am still here.

Sugar turned to gold—
Yesterday's memories transformed into dust.
A dancing sun caresses the ancient sky
until she settles peacefully in the distance,
and I am still here—beautiful in Brooklyn.

The Battle

The battle began within
in a space between the harvest hut
and a bed of burnt pumpkin leaves.

Astounded!
The village watched as a boy
desperately stole a virgin from the stone crafter's hut.
The boy insisted he loved her!
But with empty hands and broken shoes,
her father rejected his plea.
So, the boy stole the virgin
to announce and seal his love.

Villagers woke up to the shouting
of the stone crafter's hammer beating on a makeshift door.
And so, the battle began within,
in the space between a man's cry and a father's fury.
Protesting her innocence, the girl watched
her father's fury and stubbornly clung
to her lover's hand. The listeners
paced through burnt pumpkin leaves
before erupting into a torrent of snickers

"Do you understand the worth
of a daughter, the value of a virgin,
for you to appear here with empty
hands and broken shoes?"
The village roared in laughter
as the father's hammer chased the couple's love.
Thus, the battle began within
in the space between a father's dreams
and a captivated man's desires.

Knock-Kneed Love

A knock-kneed girl with moth-bitten skin
fell in love.
The object of her desire:
a dimple-kissed boy,
six feet tall with pearly white teeth.
He lived behind Ricky's Ice Cream Shack.
She visited day after day
until he forgot the knock of her knees
and saw past her moth-bitten skin.

Their romance stole a city's attention.
Confounded boys watched in wonder.
Single girls snickered
at the unconventional union.
But day after day,
the knock-kneed girl silently walked through the chatter
toward the house behind Ricky's Ice Cream Shack.

Years passed, romance became marriage.
A union birthing fourteen children.
New skin erased the moth-bitten layer
and the weight of womanhood turned the girl's knees –
until her legs straightened out!
Age stole the man's pearly white teeth,
and time forced his six feet into a quiet hunch.
But day after day, he ran home to his wife
until she forgot his thinning hair,
and saw past his hunching back.

Fifty Forevers

Before Earth was formed, I loved you.
In the heat of Sun's birth, I saw
you only. From the projects of Brooklyn
to struggling storehouses in Bronx,
seated in a rusty blue Bugatti la Voiture,
we clung to one another
and promised fifty forevers.

I loved you in the evening
when I couldn't see you in the dark,
waiting beneath a shattered streetlamp,
hidden
from an unforgiving storm. We lay
broken on the couch and buried your dream.
Our voices gave way to silence, tears
claiming our territory.
You held my hand in the confusion
until your laughter broke through Day Spring's dawn.
I loved you before the stars danced
and the sun giggled in awe
when you already loved me,
and promised fifty forevers.

To: Wandada

To Wananda,
the apple of my eye,
sugar-infused spice.
Your presence sweetens today's bitterness.
Passionate and flavorful,
honey-drenched lyrics pouring forth —
unrestrained
subtle
enrapturing
breath.
Your voice is powerful yet gentle
lacing the world in your rhymes and reasons,
enticing my senses with every beat of your flow
You move the moment.
Feet stuttering to the sound of my heart's melody
you've wrapped me in the wings of your love,
thoughtful and humble,
a man wading through many obstacles
and carrying love.
To Wananda,
my love, the apple of my moment.
Your love has birthed a song in me.

*Wandada: literal translation — the one I want

Making Love

You tasted my laughter in the dark
and held my hand on the crossroads of life.
We created love.
When we gazed at a star-drenched sky
and sang about our moment, your presence
was making love to me.
Crying in my arms, your tears
formed love. In the morning,
you woke up laughing at life.
We baked cornbread on Auntie Annie's coal stovetop
and drank chocolate milkshakes outside Ricky's Ice Cream Shack.
Side by side, walking on the shores of life,
dancing to chattering rain, you whispered
into my form, I danced
holding onto petals of your voice.
In a tottering canteen, we ate mango blossoms
watching blue butterflies chasing flame lilies
You lay next to me in the dark
and held my hand.
That moment.
This moment,
right now, is us
making love again.

Dream and Nightmare

The night Dream met Nightmare,
she shuddered.
On that fateful day, Nightmare pranced
through the shadows and entered the garden,
propping himself at the gate's entrance.
He appeared on the trail of honey marigold clusters
beneath an archway of sweet pea blossoms
and showering willow trees,
blocking the way to Visions and Joy.

"This is my world," Dream protested.
"Our world." Nightmare roared in laughter. "I exist too!"
Dream stood firm and pointed to the sky.
"I create pretty houses with beautiful gardens.
Shelters, security, food, and clothing of petals," she insisted.
"Yes, you do." Nightmare laughed and moved
swiftly, trampling on a bed of rambling roses.

"I'll fight in the morning through Day's daybreak," Dream announced.
Nightmare leapt into the sky and blocked
the sun's brilliant rays.
"You're simply an illusion." Dream wept, picking up a bruised rose.
"So are you." Nightmare chuckled. "I wonder which of us will win this
game."
He leapt to his feet and rushed back to the gate.

The night Dream met Nightmare,
a battle erupted in the very place imagination awakens
and the seeds for tomorrow are planted.

Growing

Like babies,
we hunger for experience to grow.
The milk life offers us
has its limits.
Experience becomes a father,
an ancient conversation,
guiding,
chastising
comforting—
a welcoming cradle.

Like an eagle,
swift and unexpected, life sweeps in,
chasing us out of Experience's nest—
a whirlwind,
twirling,
breaking and reconstructing.
Our efforts, weaknesses, and achievements
expose hidden purpose
and challenge Destiny's birth,
disrupting deception while establishing fears,
but with every whirl,
we grow a little older.

The Visitor

Trouble came in the form of a woman
defeating the shout of the harvest drum.
She appeared one morning
without gift or explanation.
The woman staggered past village elders,
Ignoring the twenty years they'd "raised" her grandmother,
visiting the old woman on stormy nights
while secretly grabbing half the harvest crop as compensation.
She appeared one morning,
purposed yet broken,
stealthy but bold,
until her knuckles rattled on a splinted front door.

Confusion came in the form of a whisper.
The woman leaned into an ear
and divulged the reason for her visit.
A word,
careful yet strong,
shattering decades of village protocol,
forcing the elders to abandon their seats
and meet in a secluded field.

Conflict came in the form of a letter
that the woman delivered to the village elders
at the conclusion of their sunrise meeting.
"I have a son now." The woman rose to her feet.
"He was born in the season of rain showers."
She stood in the center of the meeting.
"Today, I'm taking back my grandmother
and the harvest you confiscated for decades."

Village Gathering

The village gathered
beneath the Baobab Mango Grove tree at dawn.
A boy had fallen!
Strangers dragged his form
through the miry mud.
Named Rich by his mother
and a village elder.
Born in 1972, the boy hungered
to go to school. But Rich was black,
and a black boy should never learn to stand,
let alone read!
Strangers who ruled the town pushed him,
dragged his being through the wretched mud,
then hung his body too far to find.

At dawn, the village gathered
under the Baobab mango grove tree.
A fire stirred through restrictions of segregation.
"How many more black boys birthed to fall?"
Frustration rose
and erupted into the shattering huts.
A boy fell, so a village rose,
and the war against centuries
of segregation broke out!

Mukai* Zimbabwe

Zimbabwe, breadbasket of Africa,
peace reignite your gates.
Heart of Southern Africa—
Mukai, rise up!
Relentlessly, plow your glory again.
Harare, Sunshine City,
bury your weeping.
Abandon the unspeakable calamities,
and resist confusion.
Mukai, Mukai!
Rise up!
Breadbasket of Africa,
let prosperity invade your streets and fruitfulness rest in your farms.
Eat—your laughter resonates
throughout the universe.
Flourish.
Be full again, Zimbabwe.
Let passion's fire harvest your homes.
Then I hear a voice from heaven decree:
"Bless you, Zimbabwe.
Bless you, Zimbabwe.
Bless you, Zimbabwe."
God bless you, Zimbabwe.

*Mukai: wake up or rise up.

You

From the beginning, You were my choice,
the unequivocal answer to every need.
"Light be!"
Into the raptures of my familiar,
You burst forth.
Settling my feet in unquenchable laughter,
shattering the confines of my hidden fears,
brighter than the morning dawn,
Your Glory rested on me,
Spirit hovering over every storm.
Into Your magnificent presence, I fell,
molded in Truth.
Your word formed me.
From the beginning, You were
joyful wonders
my constant companion
in the deep and hidden places—
My Father,
my friend.
Bread of life,
eternally Elohim,
unquestionably God.

The King's Letter: Makhosini's Song*

I'm the cool breeze on a hot summer night,
hungry soil for tears of rain,
an overflowing fountain on thirsty land—
a ray of hope.
That melody of promise
at the completion of every day.
Strong!
Resilient
oak tree standing through brittle winters,
harmonizing with quiet melodies of aging spinsters.
I've withstood the test of time
and overcome pain's twisted mockery
Yes, I'm the very thought
behind your sweetest smile.
Honey to your laughter,
bread to your butter,
sugar in the season of hunger.
It's me, Makhosini Moyo—
I'm that brother.

*Makhosini Moyo: King of the Heart

Dear Reader

I hope you enjoyed your journey through Powers of Petals. I have had the pleasure of reading and writing poetry for decades. In recent years my work has expanded into Urban Poetry. Urban Poetry is a new but rapidly growing genre. It is my pleasure to share my journey through "Powers Of Poetry" with you the reader. Additionally, for your reading pleasure, I have included an expert (the first three chapters) from my debut coming-of-age novel, "When Love Danced." I hope you enjoy this too.

Yours Truly,

Mukai Jaravaza

When Love Danced

A Novel

by

Mukai Heather Jaravaza

Chapter One
Foundation: Daniel's Poem

"Before I met you, Danai, I loved you!" Daniel murmured to himself. He grimaced at summer's oppressive heat. A subtle breeze tickled his lips. He shifted uncomfortably, remembering the first time he'd laid eyes on the unusual girl.

It had been a day like today. Arthur agreed to meet him outside Ricky's Ice Cream Shack, but as usual, his cousin had been late. Daniel stood at the edge of the ice cream courtyard, silently cursing his cousin's tardiness. His gaze fell on three girls seated at a wooden table. A girl in a red minidress leaned over the tottering table and unabashedly licked her friend's ice cream cone. Bewildered, her friend pushed the girl away, but the daring girl tried a second time. Ice cream on her tongue, she burst into a smile and laughed triumphantly.

"Danai, stop!" her friend protested. Reaching toward the sky, the girl's arms shook in victory. She rose from her seat and began dancing, her hips rhythmically twirling and twisting to the beat of her rebellion.

Daniel laughed at her friend's baffled expression. Aroused with curiosity, his eyes trailed the contours of the mischievous girl's apple-shaped face. Her stubborn cheekbones arched firmly beneath small almond eyes. His gaze rested on her voluptuous lips smudged in deep red lipstick. From across the courtyard, Daniel watched and saw only her. In that moment, he had known this girl was created to be his.

"Hey, I'm here." Arthur stumbled through a growing crowd, pulling Daniel out of thoughts of the past and back into the present. "What's got you so caught up? You didn't even hear me calling." Arthur's eyes followed his cousin's gaze toward a cluster of girls gathered around DJ Tonite's turntables. His attention fell on the girl dressed in a cropped stonewashed jacket.

"Hey, isn't that the girl from Ricky's Ice Cream Shack two months ago?" He grinned at the girl's tiny denim skirt revealing her shapely cinnamon legs. "That's her, right? Hey, man, you should go talk to her." Arthur led his cousin farther into Suzette's backyard.

"Suzette, I'm sorry I'm late." Arthur jerked around to embrace a girl creeping up behind him.

"You're always late, Arthur." Suzette pouted and wrapped her arms around Arthur's waist. "How can you be late for my birthday? When are you going to grow up?"

"You know I'm trying, babe." He wiped the sweat gathering on his forehead and shoved a sloppily wrapped gift box into his girlfriend's hands. "Do you know how much I love you? Happy birthday, Suzy."

37

Oblivious to Authur and Suzette's flirtatious banter, Daniel watched the girl in the denim skirt. Two months ago, he'd been afraid to speak to her, but today Daniel felt new. "My entire life depends on this moment," he mumbled to himself, gliding toward the group of girls.

"Will you dance with me?" Daniel held out his hand. His eyes flickered to Arthur laughing in the distance.

"What?" Danai stared at the boy standing before her. Her eyes trailed down his overwashed jeans to the worn-out sandals.

"I want to dance with you," the lanky boy whispered, placing his hand in hers. Despite her friends' collective murmuring, Danai followed him to the dance floor. They moved awkwardly until Daniel set the pace, and the first song merged into the next.

Years before Danai and Daniel's paths first crossed, Daniel had become entrapped in an average existence. He couldn't remember if he chose it or it chose him. The first child of an ordinary couple who'd birthed typical dreams—a comfortable house in a nice neighborhood, a large backyard and two children—Daniel Munya Tashaya attended conventional schools and made unremarkable friends. By the time puberty arrived, he'd adopted a mediocre personality to match the commonness suffocating him. "Dependable!" He chuckled at his mother's description of him.

Startled, Danai's eyes flickered. That's when Daniel saw it—the something he couldn't explain. Danai giggled, and Daniel grinned giddily. The soft melody of her laughter ripped through him and settled into his core. The second song faded away.

"Thank you." She pulled her hand out of his grasp.

"There's this new movie, *Do the Right Thing*," he blurted out. "If you're free next Saturday, maybe we could see it together."

"I don't know you." Confusion covered Danai's face.

"A friend of mine works at Rainbow Movie Theaters, and he got me free tickets," he lied. His voice trailed off as he glanced at her friends laughing in the distance. "And I want to see it with you."

The sincerity in the boy's eyes stole Danai's attention. Reaching into a pink clutch, she pulled out an old piece of newspaper and scribbled her phone number. She shoved it into his pocket before rushing back to her friends.

She's forgotten me even before I introduced myself. Daniel watched the rhythmic sway of Danai's hips as she walked away.

"Arthur," he hollered.

"What?"

"I feel average dying and the beginning of something new," Daniel shouted. Both boys turned to gawk at the girl swaying in the distance.

Chapter Two
"Say Something"

"Yes, I'm the man, and I'm stepping out to meet the woman of my dreams," Daniel announced to his younger brother while spraying Palmer's Oil Sheen onto his fresh box cut. "Saturday, March eighteenth, 1989. Man, I will never forget this day." He grinned at a coffee-stained calendar on his dresser and shifted his attention back to the mirror reflection of himself in his favorite outfit: stone-washed jeans, a black Run-DMC T-shirt, and sky-blue Reebok high-tops. He grabbed a jacket off the dresser and rushed out of the door.

Drenched in anticipation of Spike Lee's new joint, young and old couples, crews in their best gear, and the occasional lone person clamored as they headed into Rainbow Movie Theater. The crowd appeared intoxicated with expectancy. Daniel clutched his tickets and waded through the swarm. He stood next to an elderly man at the entrance and waited for Danai. Electrified by the atmosphere, Daniel barely noticed the first hour come and go. A group of bystanders migrated to a nearby Bhawa to have a beer or two. The mass gathering dispersed into the aging theater, and Daniel frantically searched the dwindling crowd.

Do The Right Thing began, but Danai was nowhere in sight.

Daniel stood at the theater entrance until the day's heat became unbearable. An uncomfortable nakedness of rejection crept through his body. Summer's midday sun disappeared into a darkening sky. Heaven opened her mouth and soaked the earth with tears of rain. Alarmed by the rain's intensity, a heavyset woman grabbed her child and dashed toward a nearby shelter. In her haste, the woman fell onto Daniel, hurling both him and her child into gushing waters. Soaked in humiliation, Daniel rose up and trudged back home.

"I will never wait for you again, Danai," he yelled at the turbulent sky as he shoved open the familiar pink rusty gate. The boisterous rain abruptly stopped, and summer's sun reappeared as if she'd never left. Daniel stared at retreating clouds in confusion. On Saturday, March eighteenth, 1989, Daniel Munya Tashaya walked into the Tashaya home and quietly stepped back into the suffocating confines of an ordinary life.

"It's been *two weeks* since that girl stood you up. Get over it, man." Arthur barged into Daniel's bedroom and stared at the mess of unworn clothes strewn around the room. Daniel lay sprawled on his bed with his head buried under the blanket.

"Cousin, I'm taking you down under to Sarchies today." Arthur ignored his cousin's disheveled appearance and chuckled at his bewildered expression.

41

Sarchies, a rite of passage for Harare's cool crowd. An exclusive nightclub located in the hidden underground of Harare's prestigious Business District. At night, the club hosted shady events, but on Friday and Saturday afternoons, it catered to teenagers. However, the club's teens-only afternoon policy couldn't deter party-hungry university students or the disgruntled young adult working crowd. It was common to see a fifty-year-old sugar daddy searching for his fourth or fifth wife.

"Today you'll finally enter Arthur's kingdom." Arthur gulped down a glass of Mazowe juice. Daniel frowned at his cousin's description of the infamous joint. Ripe with dubious transactions, dealers used Sarchies' loud music and dim lights to camouflage their illegal activities. Dressed in elegant Pierre Cardin suits, these gentlemen of the streets engaged in everything from money laundering to luxury vehicle theft and sales. Despite the club's popularity and large weekly turnout, admittance was by invite only. A member had to invite and bring you in, vouching for your presence. No one really understood how anyone became a member, but the huge bouncers seemed to instinctively know who not to let in. Daniel vividly remembered a rumor of a girl who had been stabbed by an angry ex-lover in Sarchies. The incident took place publicly on the dance floor. When the police arrived, not one witness could be found. What happened in Sarchies stayed in Sarchies.

"So, you coming, man?" Arthur stuck his head out of the kitchen.

"Yes. I'm coming," Daniel conceded.

Dressed in black pleated pants and shiny patent leather shoes, the boys arrived in Harare's Business District shortly after noon. Arthur scrutinized his cousin and laughed. Both cousins were good-looking seventeen-year-olds but exact opposites. At five foot ten, Daniel was tall, dark, and athletically built. Shorter and stouter in stature, Arthur's round face was interrupted by a single dimple. Their differences extended to their personalities. Always popular, Arthur remained outgoing while Daniel's presence tended to go unnoticed.

"Masikati. How can I help you today?" asked a petite young woman dressed in an elaborate emerald-green suit. She sat behind a desk.

"Arthur Rwizi and guest. We are going down under," Arthur announced.

The woman pulled out a massive logbook and scanned through its withered pages. "Go ahead." She pressed a buzzer, and Daniel followed Arthur down a spiral of marble stairs. As the boys descended the stairs, they were met by the sounds of De La Souls' "Eye Know." Their journey ended at two mahogany doors flanked by four burly bouncers.

"Ah, this is Daniel. He's cool." Arthur slid the four-dollar cover charge through a small peephole. "I'm bringing him in."

An elderly white lady sat on the other side of the hole. She stuck out her hand to grab the money and stamp each boy's hand.

"Welcome down under, cousin," Arthur shouted. The bouncers opened the doors. "Welcome to Arthur's kingdom," Arthur laughed.

Elaborately furnished with black leather sofas, dark carpets, and elegant mahogany tables, Sarchies held a sense of grandeur. Daniel's eyes rapidly assessed his new surroundings. The club's classic decoration sharply contrasted beams of colorful illuminating lights that danced in tune with the music. Together it created an appealing ambience, and Daniel instinctively knew he wanted to stay.

Smoke lingered, creating an atmosphere of mystery. Amid the teens' familiar faces were dealers with their girlfriends, as well as the entire St.

43

Vincent High basketball team dressed in their customary red, gray, and white. Pretty girls in colorful outfits filled every corner. A pregnant girl breezed past as she led her partner to the dance floor, and Daniel followed Arthur, attempting to look like he belonged.

"Hey, look, there's the Richlorne crew." Arthur rushed toward the VIP seating area. Known as the Richlorne crew after the high school they attended, the group of boys ran Harare's party scene. Nyika Tumai, the group's leader, stood in the center talking to a tall girl with a short, cropped afro. The ebony beauty wore a tight-fitting short pink dress. Her rhinestone-studded heels exaggerated her height. She appeared engrossed in every word Nyika spoke.

"Hey, Nyika, this is my cousin, Danny," Arthur blurted.

The girl frowned at the unwelcome intrusion. Nyika Tumai grinned and nodded briefly before returning to his conversation with the ebony beauty. Arthur led Daniel farther into the VIP area. The rest of the Richlorne crew sat on the leopard skin couches—Godfrey, Derek Love, Will B., and of course, Makhosini Moyo. While the boys sipped on Fantas and nodded to De La Soul's "Eye Know," Makhosini's attention remained glued on something in the distance. Mesmerized and motionless, the boy gaped toward the opposite end of the club. Daniel's eyes followed Makhosini's gaze, and there she was: Danai.

Danai looked different. She'd shaved the left side of her head. The remaining hair extensions fell like a waterfall of flowing curls. Draped in a long purple dress, she moved like the wind. The music swirled, and Danai followed in twirls. The two slits on her dress opened to reveal weathered, stonewashed jeans and shiny black lace-up schoolboy shoes. The beat rocked. Danai spun. Her feet moved to every bounce of the music. Despite the club's dim ambiance, the crowd froze in awe. Oblivious to the appreciative stares, Danai flowed like a waterfall. Her arms gracefully rose upward, seeming to capture each delicious sound.

When the song ended, she simply left the dance floor and sat on a couch next to one of her friends. Daniel glanced back at Makhosini, whose attention was elsewhere. Still captivated, Daniel glided toward Danai.

"Hi," he blurted.

Surprised, Danai glanced up at the lanky boy in a Run-DMC T-shirt. She burst into a fit of giggles. Daniel grinned and forgot he'd ever stood in the rain waiting for her.

Chapter Three
Invitation

"Where are we going?" Danai shouted, twirling on the street corner. Her eyes slanted to avoid summer's piercing sun rays, and Daniel laughed. "Is that for me?" she asked.

A vision of Arthur's expression when he'd confessed that he'd asked Danai out again floated through his mind. *Be careful, man.* His cousin's warning resonated in his thoughts.

Daniel had arrived early for their date, carrying a blossoming blue orchid. To his delight, Danai showed up on time this time.

"Is that for me?" she asked again.

"Yes."

"I love orchids." She beamed in delight and hugged the miniature pot. "Thank you, Daniel."

"Follow me, Miss Matamba." He grabbed her hand and led the way to the spectacular, newly renovated Flame Lilly Inn.

"I keep hearing this song everywhere." Danai settled into a booth by the window.

"Oh, that's 'The Way Love Is' by Ten City. That whole album is totally off the wall," Daniel said, sitting opposite her. "It's about this guy and girl who meet. They fall in love and promise each other forever. The crazy part is that things go wrong. Their love suddenly dies, and they go separate ways."

"Really." Danai watched him carefully. "Have you ever been in love?"

"No, not yet." Daniel grinned. "And you? Am I going to be your first love?"

"What?" She erupted in laughter. They launched into a discussion on love and music: the greatest hits, missed number ones, and the songs they both thought were simply overrated. A waitress appeared and took their orders.

"So, Daniel, what do you do for fun?"

"Well, there's not much to tell," he mumbled. His ordinary existence flickered through his mind. "What about you? Do you have any siblings?"

"I do." Danai smiled, ignoring his forlorn expression, "I have a nine-year-old brother, Miles. He's my cuddly annoyance."

They ate in silence with Daniel peering over his food at Danai, while she glared at other patrons. Despite her enjoying her food, the delicious meal was marked with an awkward tension. Determined to lighten the mood, Daniel joked about a date he had gone on a month earlier.

47

"So, she showed up an hour late with five of her friends. Before I sat down, her five friends had picked out the most expensive things on the menu and were demanding I pay for their meals." Daniel shook his head, laughing. "So, I sat down, quickly gulped down my meal, and then I snuck out through the back door." He chuckled at his own ingenuity.

Danai frowned but nodded silently.

"So, Danai, what do you think about me?" He nervously swallowed.

Danai slowly chewed. "I think you're being a typical seventeen-year-old boy."

"What do you mean?"

"You're very predictable." Her eyes wandered from his gaze to his plate.

"Well, I am an average guy." He shifted uncomfortably. "So, what are you saying?"

"I'm saying that it's a hot day but you had us walk up and down First Street for an hour so everyone would see us." She played with a roasted potato. "Now you are telling me about some girl I'll probably never meet. That's typical." She lifted her knife and sliced her potato into tiny pieces. They ate the rest of the meal in silence.

"Okay, so why don't you pick the next place we go to?" Daniel suggested as they left Flame Lilly Inn. "Maybe we could do something not typical." Despite Danai's earlier comments, he'd enjoyed their date and wanted to see her again.

"Daniel, you really seem like a nice guy, but I don't think this is for me. I . . ."

"I like you, Danai." He nervously ran his fingers through his hair. "A lot."

"I think you like the idea of us."

"Yes, I like that, too. I want everything, girl." He grinned at her expression. "Give me one more chance. We'll go where you want to go and do something you like. And if it doesn't work out, then we'll just go separate ways."

The following Saturday, Daniel rushed into Rick's Ice Cream Shack and found Danai waiting for him.

"Hi." She waved and adjusted the strap on her faded indigo-wash overalls. "Are you ready, Danny?"

Weaving through streams of pedestrians while avoiding traffic, Daniel followed Danai past several high-rise buildings. At the entrance of the overly populated Material District, Danai stood on the edge of a curb and stuck out her thumb. A speeding minivan came to a halt.

"Come on, let's go." She pushed into the crowded van.

Daniel squeezed between a large woman in a tight orange skirt and a young schoolboy. "Where are we going?" Daniel asked.

"Mbare. Mbare Musika. Let's go," bellowed the boy who manned the door. The boy stuck half his body out of the moving vehicle and continued shouting at anyone walking in the direction the van was heading.

Mbare Musika! Was this one of Danai's silly pranks? Daniel's unanswered question sparked internal panic.

Built during the oppressive segregation era of colonization, Mbare lay at the city's outskirts. Initially a close-knit settlement for migratory farmers, Mbare transformed into a bustling bus center built to transport Black people to any part of the country they worked. Within weeks, multiple food stands appeared. With the stands came eager street vendors who sold everything from ladies' shoes and children's clothing to farming equipment. Amid the confusion, a massive flourishing marketplace erupted, and the tiny settlement transformed into a thriving township.

Despite the end of colonialism and several changes in the country, Mbare remained standing: solid and proud. Mbare's doctors and professors moved to more affluent suburbs, and the once attractive surroundings deteriorated into decaying apartment flats that housed everything from struggling families to seasoned thieves. People were born in Mbare, and they died in Mbare. That was the story of their life. Like most suburban teens in Zimbabwe, Daniel had heard about Mbare Musika but never been there. He was surprised Danai knew how to get there.

"Give me your wallet, Daniel." Danai held out her hand as the minivan came to a halt. Danai paid the boy who manned the door, and Daniel followed her out of the van into the unruly marketplace. His eyes danced at the sights surrounding him: women selling vegetables, new and used clothes, curtains, and handcrafted furniture.

"Come and buy them now. They'll be gone tomorrow!" A man enticed customers. Daniel grinned at the man's brazen display of the latest BeatBoxes. Old women purchased sewing machines, and young mothers bought their weekly food supply. A group of enthusiastic tourists bargained with a vendor for his overpriced glistering Shona sculptures, and a savvy businessman grinned triumphantly as he rushed past the couple.

Danai stopped at a staggering hut with corroding metal roofing and read the rusty blackboard: "Alice's Shabeen." The hut's entrance gave a clear view of metal plates, jars of spices, and preserved foods. Outside, thirty wooden crates had been converted into seats for customers. A large firewood stove with black pots lay in the center. A woman wiped her sooty hands on her worn apron and greeted Danai.

"This is Mai Chenai," Danai told Daniel. "Or Alice. She's the owner." She handed Mai Chenai fifty cents, and the woman hurried into the hut, opened a mini fridge, and returned with bottles of ginger ale and cherry plum.

Around the shabeen's periphery, African batiks, oil paintings, and other pieces of art hung on chicken wire fence.

"So, what do you think?" Danai pointed to a medium-sized painting depicting a peaceful village setting. In the center of the serene setting stood a young girl in a tattered green dress defiantly holding a book.

Daniel walked up to the oil painting and took a closer look. The artist had inscribed her name at the bottom of the canvas. "You did this?" he blurted in astonishment.

"Yes, I did!" Danai giggled. "I bring my stuff here. Cautious, Mai Chenai's oldest son, collects and sells art. He sells some of my paintings."

Upon hearing his name, Cautious suddenly appeared. Dressed in a wrinkled shirt and unwashed jeans, he stood glaring suspiciously at Daniel.

Ignoring Cautious, Danai asked, "Daniel, are you hungry?"

"Yeah, I am."

"Okay, come. Let's eat."

They joined twenty other guests seated on crates. A teenage girl wearing a sauce-stained apron hovered over everyone. Pouring water

51

into a basin, she allowed each customer to wash their hands. Mai Chenai followed, unloading bowls of steaming sadza and steak into her customers' hungry hands. As Daniel became aware of the inviting spicy aroma, he heard his stomach growl in anticipation. He reached for one of Mai Chenai's bowls and gulped down his sadza. The simple meal was delicious.

A man in a faded sky-blue suit leaned over and declared, "A steak is never a steak without *Chibuku*." He handed Daniel a container of Mai Chenai's thick brown homemade brew. Daniel took a sip and passed it to Danai.

She frowned and stared at the container. "Nope, and if you're clever, you won't either."

While the customers dug into their meals, the man in the faded blue suit began his story. Everyone listened and occasionally commented as the man talked about his woes and the battles between his two wives. In a relaxed mood, he recounted how he met and fell in love with his first wife. "We were like you two." The man pointed at Daniel and Danai. "I was seventeen, and she was just fifteen. I knew she was the one the first time I laid eyes on her." The man smiled and reminisced about how they left the village and moved to the city. He began working for a manufacturing company, and his wife became a schoolteacher. The years unfolded with promotion after promotion until he became the company's general manager. "Sometimes life doesn't work out the way you plan it." The man shook his head and chuckled. A few customers nodded in agreement. "I felt I needed to take on a second wife. It was an act of mercy. I wanted to share the wealth," the man declared, and the crowd convulsed with laughter.

"I'm a prisoner." Lucky Dube's melodious voice penetrated through Mai Chenai's wireless radio. "I'm a prisoner," Lucky moaned. The man in the blue suit gulped his Chibuku and shook his head at the irony.

"I married for love." A disheveled woman in a traditional head scarf settled onto a crate and began her story. "My mother and aunts warned me to marry in wisdom, but I scoffed at their foolishness and married for love. My husband and I, we started out that way, with me loving him and him simply living in the moment." The woman adjusted her head wrap while the crowd hummed in anticipation.

"To make love work, I worked hard as a housemaid. Cleaning other people's bedrooms and chasing after their insolent children while my own home remained unkept, and my daughters grew up seeing their mother once a month." The woman laughed boldly, exposing a missing tooth. Surprised, Daniel moved closer.

"I'm a grown woman but every day I bow to women younger than me. I call them Madame, and they label me girl." The woman's voice trailed off as the crowd quivered in bitterness. Mai Chenai moved around, discretely serving each customer while the crowd continued listening intently.

"I didn't mind because I married for love. While my husband gambled our meager savings and neglected our home, I woke up each day and kept bowing to those young girls who'd married in wisdom." The woman rose to her feet. With her hands clasping her head, she slowly paced between the crates.

"Last week, my husband's family came to visit our home. They brought a young girl in her twenties. I rejoiced, believing they'd finally heard my pain and brought me my own housemaid. I eagerly sat on the

53

floor and served my in-laws. 'You can rest now,' my father-in-law cheered and ate greedily. 'You birthed four beautiful girls, but we need a son. We've bought a new madam for your home to take on that task.' Astonished, I turned to my husband, and that's when I realized, I'd married for love, and he was now happily living in this moment."

"Oh no, what to do?" The crowd's muffled dismay filtered the woman's agony.

Defeated, the woman dropped to the ground and sat in the dust.

"How can this be?" An elderly man leaned on his cane and angrily spat into the air. Customers shook their heads and resumed eating in silence.

Breaking the silence, a different person shared his own story, while a separate group formed to discuss Zimbabwe's current politics. Daniel listened and giggled. He'd forgotten his surroundings. He felt strangely comfortable and was enjoying himself. He felt good, like he was floating.

"That's the Chibuku." He heard Danai's warning. "And it's getting dark. Time to go." She rose from her crate and handed Mai Chenai the dollars for their meal.

"How much for this one?" Daniel motioned to Cautious and pointed at Danai's work of art.

"Thirty dollars."

"What? Cautious, have you lost your mind?" Mai Chenai's head swerved toward her son. "Do you want me to interrupt your stupidity with a good slap?"

"Twenty dollars," the young man conceded.

"Give me my wallet," Daniel ordered Danai. He pulled out his last note and handed it to Cautious.

"Hey, man, wake up. Wake up, man. We're here!" A male voice dragged Daniel out of his sleep. He grudgingly opened his eyes. Slouched in the back seat of a taxi, he clung to the painting of the girl in the green dress but couldn't find his wallet or Danai.

"I think I was robbed," Daniel stuttered in embarrassment as he slid out of the taxicab, "I'll pay you tomorrow," he assured the taxi driver, who hurled angry insults. Ignoring the driver's threats, he staggered through the rusty pink gate and into his home. Confused but still hugging his painting, he walked past his parents and into his bedroom. With Danai's art propped on his chest, Daniel dropped onto his bed and fell back asleep.

www.ingramcontent.com/pod-product-compliance
Lightning Source LLC
Chambersburg PA
CBHW031007090426
42737CB00008B/724